# TRUE or FALSE?

This meal could make you sick.

D0005215

# TRUE!

## (But unlikely!)

About 150 people have died from an illness called mad cow disease. If this burger were made from an infected cow, you could get sick. Very sick.

But the disease is rare. And scientists and other experts work hard to make sure that contagious diseases like mad cow don't spread through the population.

Want to know more? Keep reading.

Book design Red Herring Design/NYC

Library of Congress Cataloging-in-Publication Data
DiConsiglio, John.
When birds get flu and cows go mad! : how safe are we? / by John DiConsiglio.
p. cm. — (24/7: science behind the scenes)
Includes bibliographical references.
ISBN-13: 978-0-531-12069-9 (lib. bdg.)   978-0-531-17528-6 (pbk.)
ISBN-10: 0-531-12069-4 (lib. bdg.)   0-531-17528-6 (pbk.)
1. Zoonoses—Juvenile literature. I. Title.
RC113.5.D53 2007
616.9'59—dc22   2006006810

10/07 6  26.00 ~ 16.90

# WHEN BIRDS GET FLU AND COWS GO MAD!

## How Safe Are We?

John DiConsiglio

**WARNING:** You'll need a strong stomach to gobble down the true stories about barnyard animals in this book.

**Franklin Watts**
An Imprint of Scholastic Inc.
New York • Toronto • London • Auckland • Sydney
Mexico City • New Delhi • Hong Kong
Danbury, Connecticut

# CONTENTS

These cases are 100% real. Find out how doctors and other health experts solved these deadly mysteries.

**15** Case #1:
## The Mystery of the Killer Bird Flu!

**An 11-year-old girl and her mother die from a serious flu. Is this the start of a worldwide health crisis?**

Scientists track a killer flu in Thailand.

**29** Case #2:
## The Case of the Missing Mad Cow!

**A single sick cow slips into the food supply. Can one animal cause a national health emergency?**

Has beef in Washington State been contaminated?

# MEDICAL DOWNLOAD

*This amazing stuff is nothing to sneeze at.*

Say a person dies from a really bad disease. And no one knows what kind it was.

## MEDICAL 411

That's a job for experts in infectious diseases. They'll study the person's blood and body fluids. They'll examine where the victim lived. They'll try to identify the disease and stop it from claiming more lives.

### IN THIS SECTION:

- ▶ how health experts really talk;
- ▶ a close-up look at bird flu and mad cow disease;
- ▶ and who else studies and treats infectious diseases.

# What's the Word?

**Disease fighters have their own way of speaking. Find out what their vocabulary means.**

**infectious**
(in-FEK-shuhss) easy to spread from one person to another

We have a problem. She's suffering from the flu, and it's highly **infectious**.

I just got the results back from the lab. It was a **virus** that killed the cows and horses.

**virus**
(VYE-ruhss) a tiny organism that often causes disease. It's so small that scientists can only see it under a powerful microscope.

We have an **outbreak** of bird flu in the village. I'm afraid this could turn into an **epidemic**.

**outbreak**
(OUT-brake) the sudden spread of a disease in a population—like a neighborhood, school, or hospital

**epidemic**
(ep-uh-DEM-ik) an outbreak of disease that spreads quickly over a wide area and to many people

# Say What?

Epidemic? I wish that's all we were talking about! We're looking at a possible pandemic!

## pandemic
(pan-DEM-ik) an outbreak of disease that spreads to many different countries—or even the whole world

The problem is that we don't have a vaccine for this disease.

## vaccine
(vak-SEEN) an injection given to prevent a specific illness. It's usually made from a very weak version of the organism that causes the disease, so the human body can learn to fight it off.

We're going to have to put these patients in quarantine.

## quarantine
(KWOR-uhn-teen) the act of keeping people who might become sick away from healthy ones

Here's some other lingo disease hunters might use on the job.

## diagnosis
(dye-ugh-NOHS-sis) the identification of a patient's illness after doing lab tests and studying physical symptoms
*"The doctor will make a **diagnosis** once your blood tests come back from the lab."*

## hot zone
(hot zohn) a place where a disease has been detected and there's a high danger of catching it
*"We need to shut down the entire school. It's a **hot zone** for the flu."*

## mutate
(MYOO-tate) to change
*"I worry that this curable disease might **mutate** into a killer we can't stop."*

## prognosis
(prog-NOH-sis) a prediction about a patient's recovery from an illness
*"My **prognosis** is that you'll have no lasting effects from the disease."*

# Nothing to Sneeze At

**Here's a look at the symptoms of and treatments for bird flu and mad cow disease.**

## Avian Influenza
### commonly called bird flu

| symptoms | how you get it | treatment | prognosis |
|---|---|---|---|
| In its early stages, bird flu acts just like an ordinary flu. Patients might have a fever, headache, or aches and pains.<br><br>But within days, bird flu sufferers get a lot worse. They have difficulty breathing. They may also have vomiting and diarrhea. They can become delirious and may die. | Birds like chickens, turkeys, and ducks pass it to each other. They catch it from the blood, saliva, or urine of a sick bird.<br><br>Humans are most at risk if they handle chickens or live in a place where chickens are kept as pets.<br><br>Catching bird flu from another person is rare. | **Antiviral** drugs like Tamiflu and Relenza are the only treatments that seem to fight bird flu. But they have to be taken within 72 hours after a person is infected. | It's not good. Untreated, bird flu is often fatal. It kills about half of all people who are infected with it. |

# Bovine Spongiform Encephalopathy (BSE)
## commonly called mad cow disease

| symptoms | how you get it | treatment | prognosis |
| --- | --- | --- | --- |
| Cows with BSE become confused. They can't stand or walk. Their brains waste away and become spongy.<br><br>People who eat meat from infected cows develop variant Creutzfeldt-Jakob Disease (vCJD). Their brains waste away; they lose perception, memory, and judgment. Eventually, they die. | Cows can't pass BSE to each other or to humans. The only way to catch the disease is by eating infected beef.<br><br>As of spring 2007, only three cases of mad cow disease have ever been reported in the U.S. And they were all in cows. The disease is not contagious. You can't catch it from someone who is sick with it. | There is no treatment for people or cows. | There is no known cure for mad cow. In every case, it is fatal. |

## Mad Sheep?

Mad cow disease may have started with mad sheep. Cows in England were often given food that contained ground-up sheep. Mad cow resembles a sheep disease called scrapie. If scrapie got into their food, cows could have caught it.

# The Medical Team

**Health experts work as a team. Here's a look at those who fight to keep animal diseases from spreading to humans.**

### EPIDEMIOLOGISTS
They're scientists who study the health of groups of people. Some travel to places where there are outbreaks of illness. Others work in the lab to find ways to prevent diseases from occurring.

### VETERINARIANS
They are medical doctors who diagnose and treat diseases in animals.

### INTERNAL MEDICINE DOCTORS
They're doctors who treat diseases that affect the internal organs. They also prescribe drugs to help cure patients' illnesses.

### VIROLOGISTS
They're scientists who work in the lab to study diseases caused by viruses. Their goal is to find cures for people who are sick. And they try to develop vaccines to prevent others from getting sick.

### FOOD INVESTIGATORS
They're health experts who track down unsafe food to help prevent illnesses. Some work for the government. They inspect places where beef and chicken are prepared for supermarkets and restaurants.

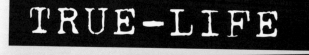

# TRUE-LIFE
# CASE FILES!

**24 hours a day, 7 days a week, 365 days a year, disease hunters are working to prevent and treat illnesses caused by animals.**

### IN THIS SECTION:

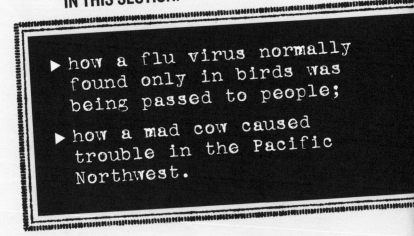

► how a flu virus normally found only in birds was being passed to people;

► how a mad cow caused trouble in the Pacific Northwest.

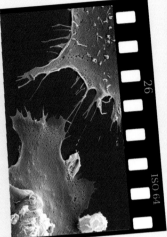

## How do disease hunters get the job done?

Each of the cases you're about to read is very different. But the steps the health experts followed are similar. These disease hunters use a scientific process to figure out what caused an illness and how to contain it. You can follow this process as you read the case studies. Keep an eye out for the icons below.

**THE QUESTION** At the beginning of each case, the disease hunters ask **one or two main questions** about the mystery.

**THE EVIDENCE** The next step is to **gather and analyze evidence**. They look for symptoms. They take samples and run tests. Then they study the evidence to figure out what it means.

**THE CONCLUSION** Along the way, they come up with theories about what may have happened. They test these theories against the evidence. Does the evidence back up the theory? **If so, they've reached a conclusion**.

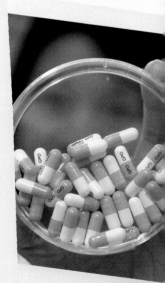

Thailand
September 2004

# The Mystery of the Killer Bird Flu!

**An 11-year-old girl and her mother die from a serious flu. Is this the start of a worldwide health crisis?**

# A Killer Strikes!

**A girl and her mother die of the flu, and experts are called to find out why.**

Dr. Kumnuan Ungchusak raced his jeep through the countryside of Thailand. He's a health official in Thailand. With him was Scott Dowell, a doctor from the United States.

The men sped by miles of rice paddies. It was extremely hot. But the two experts weren't thinking about the landscape or the weather. They had more pressing matters on their minds.

They were rushing to stop a killer before it killed again.

The two men were heading to the tiny village of Srisomboon. It was September 2004. An 11-year-old girl had fallen ill after playing with some sick chickens. At first, it seemed like a bad case of the flu. But the girl kept getting sicker.

In the hospital, her mother held her for hours. Then early in the morning, the girl died. Soon, her mother began to feel sick. The mother died, too.

A little girl in Thailand had died of avian flu after playing with some infected chickens.

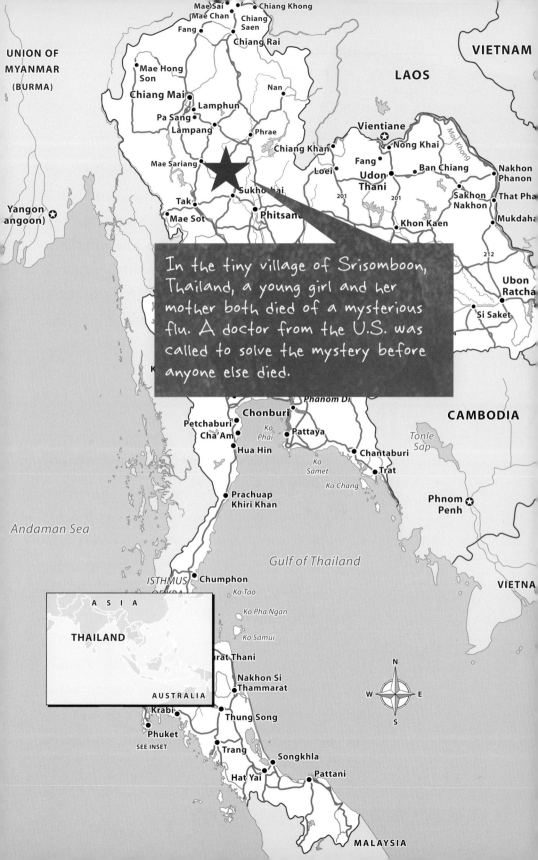

UNION OF
MYANMAR
(BURMA)

VIETNAM

LAOS

Mae Sai
Mae Chan
Chiang Saen
Chiang Khong
Fang
Chiang Rai

Mae Hong
Son

Nan

Chiang Mai
Lamphun
Pa Sang
Lampang
Phrae
Vientiane
Nong Khai

Chiang Khan
Fang
Loei
Udon
Thani
Ban Chiang
Sakhon
Nakhon
Nakhon
Phanon
That Pha

Mae Sariang
Sukho Tai
201
201
Mukdaha
Tak
Phitsan
Khon Kaen
Mae Sot

Yangon
angoon)

212

Ubon
Ratcha

Si Saket

In the tiny village of Srisomboon,
Thailand, a young girl and her
mother both died of a mysterious
flu. A doctor from the U.S. was
called to solve the mystery before
anyone else died.

Phanom Di
Chonburi
CAMBODIA
Petchaburi
Cha Am
Ko
Phai
Pattaya
Tonle
Sap
Hua Hin
Chantaburi
Ko
Samet
Trat
Ko Chang

Prachuap
Khiri Khan
Phnom
Penh

Andaman Sea

Gulf of Thailand

VIETNA

ISTHMUS
OF KRA
Chumphon
Ko Tao

ASIA

Ko Pha Ngan

THAILAND

Ko Samui

rat Thani

Nakhon Si
Thammarat

AUSTRALIA

N

Krabi
Thung Song

W        E

Phuket
SEE INSET
Trang

S

Songkhla

Hat Yai
Pattani

MALAYSIA

Epidemiologists worried that one or two sick chickens could infect a whole town. And that town could infect the country—or even the world.

Dr. Dowell is an epidemiologist. His job is to figure out what makes people sick—and to keep diseases from spreading to others.

He feared that the little girl and her mother had died from a rare bird flu.

If Dowell was right, it could mean big trouble. Not just for the little Thai town—but possibly for the whole world.

# The Disease Fighter

**Dr. Dowell has battled deadly illness before, but this case could be the worst.**

Dr. Dowell is a doctor with the Centers for Disease Control and Prevention (**CDC**) in Atlanta, Georgia. That's a U.S. government agency that tracks and combats deadly diseases around the world.

Dr. Dowell is often assigned to live in a foreign country for several years at a time. While he's there, he helps local governments solve problems that cause diseases to spread—such as bad **sanitation** and poor health care.

Dr. Scott Dowell from the CDC spoke to reporters in Thailand after health officials announced the two deaths from avian flu. It was the first probable case of person-to-person bird flu infection.

Dr. Dowell was assigned to Thailand in 2001. But before then, he battled a deadly virus called **Ebola** in Zaire, Africa. That disease was so contagious that he had to dress in protective gear that looked like a spacesuit.

And in Asia, he treated **SARS**. That's a mystery illness that has killed at least 800 people. He wore a Darth Vader-like mask to keep from inhaling the SARS germs.

In 2004, Dr. Dowell started keeping an eye on flu viruses that could spread out of control. "The next flu pandemic is one of public health's greatest concerns," he says.

That's why the deaths in the Thai village troubled him. "This has the potential to be that kind of disease," he told himself.

# DISEASE CENTRAL

**For the past 60 years, the CDC have kept an eye on the health of the world.**

"You may not know our name," a worker at the CDC says. "But you hear from us when an outbreak occurs and a quick response is needed."

The Centers for Disease Control and Prevention (CDC) is the U.S. government agency in charge of protecting public health. A key part of the agency's mission is to track and control contagious diseases.

## Mosquito Killers

The CDC started in 1946 in Atlanta, Georgia. At first, the organization focused mainly on the control of malaria—which meant killing mosquitoes. Scientists at the center organized a huge effort to spray an insecticide called DDT on more than six million homes. And by 1949, malaria was no longer a serious health problem in the U.S.

## Global Concerns

In 1958, scientists at the CDC made their first trip overseas. A team went to Southeast Asia to respond to an epidemic of smallpox and cholera.

Since then, the CDC has been active throughout the world, following infectious such as smallpox, polio, tuberculosis, **AIDS**, and SARS.

A worker from the CDC demonstrates a protective suit used during the study and treatment of the Ebola virus in 1995.

# A Medical Mystery

**Dr. Dowell's worry: Did the girl pass deadly bird flu directly to her mother?**

The disease that concerned Dr. Dowell was avian influenza, or bird flu. This virus usually strikes poultry, like chickens, ducks, and turkeys. It's rare for bird flu to make people sick.

In fact, by 2003, only about 40 people had died from bird flu in the whole world. And all of them had gotten it from handling sick birds or breathing in their **secretions**, like saliva.

In some places in Thailand, chickens run freely through homes. Some are even kept as pets. In those conditions, there's always a danger of a bird flu outbreak.

First, Dr. Dowell had to test to see if the little girl had died of bird flu she caught from the sick chickens.

More important, he had to learn if the mother had caught the flu directly from her daughter. If so, this would be the first case *ever* reported of a person passing the flu to another person.

If humans could pass the bird flu to other humans, it would be a health disaster! Bird flu could quickly spread around the globe. Anywhere a sick person traveled, he or she could make others ill—even if there were no chickens nearby.

In 2006, Thailand experienced another outbreak of bird flu. Here, a government official dressed in protective gear prepares to search a henhouse for diseased chickens. During a two-week period, about 300,000 suspect chickens were killed.

Livestock officials throw sacks of destroyed chickens into a pit in a town west of Bangkok, Thailand.

That's called a pandemic. A pandemic is a disease that spreads across many countries, or the entire world. Thousands—perhaps millions—of people could die.

Dr. Dowell had to find some answers—and fast!

# Hot Zone!

### Dr. Dowell investigates the cause of the killer disease.

The girl's body had already been **cremated**. But the mother's body was still available. Dowell waited anxiously as a fellow scientist tested a sample of her lung tissue.

Finally, Dowell's cell phone rang. As he feared, the mother had died from a deadly bird flu **strain** called **H5N1**.

The next step for Dr. Dowell and his colleagues was to determine how mother and daughter had caught the flu—and if they'd passed it on to others. The experts retraced the victims' last few hours, step-by-step.

After helping her uncle bury some dead chickens, the girl developed a stomachache and a high fever, Dowell learned. She couldn't walk and was vomiting blood.

Her mother worked nearly four hours away in Bangkok, Thailand's capital. She hurried home to look after her sick daughter.

THE EVIDENCE

She sat at her daughter's bedside. She kissed and held her through the night. Early the next morning, the young girl died. The mother soon became sick and died, too.

THE CONCLUSION

It seemed unlikely that the mother caught the flu from chickens. During her day in the hospital, she never left her daughter's room. That meant the mother most likely caught bird flu directly from her infected daughter.

Dr. Dowell knew this was big trouble. It was the first time a person had caught bird flu from another person. The virus must have changed—or mutated. It had become even more dangerous than before. Now many other people would be at risk of getting sick and dying.

Dr. Dowell hurried to see

This is an enlarged image of the avian flu virus.

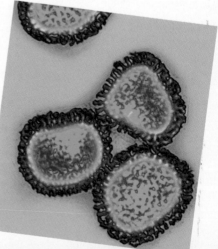

23

if anyone else from the village had been infected. An aunt and a cousin were also sick. But their cases of bird flu were mild. Dr. Dowell began treating them with an antiviral medicine called Tamiflu.

He separated them from healthy people until they were well. Luckily, the virus didn't spread through the rest of the village—or beyond.

"We dodged a bullet," Dr. Dowell says.

Tamiflu is an antiviral medicine that can help treat bird flu. But it must be given to a person within 72 hours after he or she is infected with the disease. Since 2005, governments have stockpiled Tamiflu in preparation for a possible pandemic.

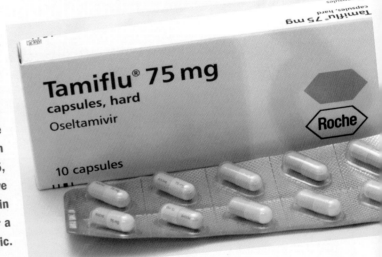

# A MUTANT FLU

**When a virus mutates, or changes, it can cause real trouble. That's why some experts fear that bird flu could become a worldwide health crisis.**

About a million people a year die from the flu. Many are elderly and already sick.

Because we've all been exposed to the flu before, most of us have built up **immunity** to it. That means our bodies recognize the flu virus when it hits us. We know how to battle it.

We also fight back with vaccines—shots of medicine that can make us immune to some viruses. Have you ever had a flu shot? That was a vaccine to protect you against certain kinds of flu.

## Changing Viruses

But there's big trouble when a virus mutates. This means it actually changes. It becomes a different virus. That makes it harder for our bodies to fight. And a vaccine may fail to work against the mutated virus.

If bird flu mutated so it could easily spread from person to person, we'd all be in danger. The World Health Organization estimates that it could kill between 2 and 7.4 million people in many different countries.

There is no way to stop a virus from mutating. The best doctors can do is try to control it once it mutates. They can create new vaccines to fight it. And they can separate—or isolate—sick people from healthy ones to keep the virus from spreading.

This is how one mutant looked in the movies. It definitely looks like a human, but there's something, well, different. Likewise, a mutant flu virus is sort of like the original flu virus. But there's something quite different.

# IS HELP ON THE WAY?

## Scientists hurry to find a vaccine for H5N1 bird flu.

Viruses have some powerful enemies— vaccines.

Many vaccines work by introducing a small dose of a harmful virus into your body. This dose is too small to hurt you—but big enough to help your body learn to fight it.

Other vaccines introduce only parts of a germ into your body— not a live germ. Still, as with the other vaccines, your body recognizes the germ and learns to fight it.

### A Bird Flu Vaccine?

Now scientists are working on vaccines to fight the deadly bird flu H5N1. But these vaccines aren't easy to make. One reason is that the flu virus often mutates. So a vaccine that worked against the flu last year won't protect you very well this year.

Another problem is that it takes years of tests to make sure bird flu vaccines will work on humans without making them sick.

In 2005, a study began testing a possible bird flu vaccine on 450 people. The vaccine uses a type of bird flu that was found in Southeast Asia in 2004. Some of the early results are promising. But as of spring 2007, there is still no vaccine available for H5N1.

One kid endures a vaccine. Many diseases have been controlled or wiped out by vaccines. Polio and smallpox are two examples.

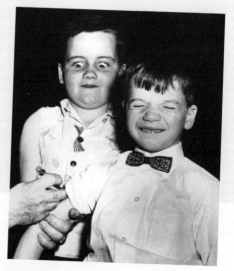

# The World Holds Its Breath

**Dr. Dowell urges countries to get prepared—and to help each other out.**

Dr. Dowell had proven that bird flu could pass from person to person. But still, it hadn't been spread easily. The mother had held her dying daughter for hours.

But Dr. Dowell—and the rest of the world—had a new worry: What happens if H5N1 mutates, or changes, again? What if it becomes easier to pass bird flu from person to person—like with just a sneeze?

If that happens, the world could face a pandemic.

Dr. Dowell says we need to be prepared for a pandemic. He thinks every nation should have an emergency plan. More medications like Tamiflu should be available. He thinks rich countries like the U.S. should help poor countries pay for medicine and health care.

"We're all in this together," he says. "This time, we stopped it. Next time, we might not be as lucky." 24/7

# THE DEADLIEST VIRUS

## In 1918, the Spanish flu killed people all over the world.

The deadliest pandemic of the last 100 years was the **Spanish flu**. It started in the fall of 1918. World War I was ending. Tired soldiers were returning to their homes.

No one imagined that another enemy was about to attack.

The Spanish flu would kill between 40 and 50 million people—more people that were killed in the war.

This pandemic affected everyone—and spread everywhere. Outbreaks swept through North America, Europe, Asia, Africa, Brazil, and the South Pacific. At one point, one-fifth of the entire globe was infected.

Returning soldiers brought this deadly virus back to their families. People died horribly. Some gasped for breath, suffocating to death. Others found their lungs flooded with blood.

And then, just as suddenly, in 1919 the Spanish flu ended.

### From the Barnyard?

So where did this killer flu come from? In 2005, researchers at the CDC announced that it had probably started off as a bird flu and then jumped to humans.

Does that sound familiar? The Spanish flu is very similar to the bird flu we see today. Some scientists believe it's the same strain of influenza. It's left them wondering: Could an illness from birds cause another flu pandemic?

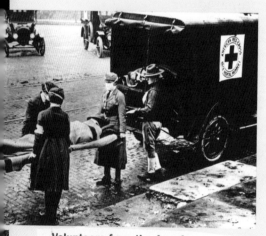

Volunteers from the American Red Cross assist victims of the Spanish flu in 1918.

In the next case, a sick cow may cause a national health disaster—unless experts work quickly to stop it.

The Pacific Northwest
December 2003

# The Case of the Missing Mad Cow!

A single sick cow slips into
the food supply. Can one
animal cause a national
health emergency?

Two days before Christmas in 2003, a cow in Washington State tested positive for mad cow disease. It was the first case ever found in the U.S. Health experts had to act fast—before any people caught the illness and died!

# Wanted: Mad Cow!

**There's a sick cow out there. And a food detective gets the call to track it down.**

The phone rang two days before Christmas.

The moment investigator Will Hughes heard what the caller had to say, he knew he was facing a deadly health emergency. A diseased cow had been found—and many lives were at risk.

Early that morning, a tissue sample from a cow in Washington State had tested positive for bovine spongiform encephalopathy (BSE)—also known as mad cow disease. That's a rare brain disorder that kills both animals and humans. In Europe, hundreds of thousands of cows have caught the disease. And 150 humans have died from it.

But mad cow disease had never appeared in the U.S.

Until now!

Hughes is an investigator for the Food and Drug Administration (**FDA**). That's the government agency that checks the safety of the food we eat. He knew that animals and people could die from eating parts of this mad cow.

Before 2003, mad cow had never been found in a U.S. cow. But in Europe, mad cow was more widespread. Here, a scientist in Germany places a sample of a cow's brain in a test tube. The sample will be analyzed for BSE.

What's more, by the time Hughes got the call, the cow's meat had already been sent to packing plants, grocery stores, and restaurants all over the region.

Hughes is like a food detective. It's his job to find these cow parts before anyone gets sick or dies.

He kissed his wife good-bye, grabbed his badge, and drove off into the night. He wouldn't be back in time to celebrate Christmas with his family. He was facing his toughest case ever.

In 2003, the beef section in this New York City supermarket was marked with caution tape after the mad cow discovery.

# HOW DO YOU MAKE A COW MAD?

## Mad cow disease is serious—but fairly rare.

You can call it mad cow disease. Or you can call it bovine spongiform encephalopathy (BSE). But by any name, it's a disorder that attacks the brain. There's no known cure—and it's always fatal.

A cow infected with BSE has difficulty holding up its head. Its muscles twitch uncontrollably. It stumbles and falls. Eventually, it loses the ability to walk. Soon after, it dies.

People who eat meat from a cow infected with BSE can have similar **symptoms**. Their brain tissue gets spongy, resulting in **dementia**. That's a nerve disorder that causes loss of perception, memory, and judgment. After a while, they become paralyzed— and then die.

### Brain Disease

The human version of mad cow resembles a rare brain disease called variant Creutzfeldt-Jakob disease (vCJD). It seems to affect mostly young adults. It strikes five or more years after the victim ate bad meat. In every case, the infected person has died.

Perhaps the best news about mad cow is that people do not catch it easily. Chances are, millions of people have eaten infected beef. But, for reasons scientists still do not understand, only about 150 people have gotten vCJD and died from it.

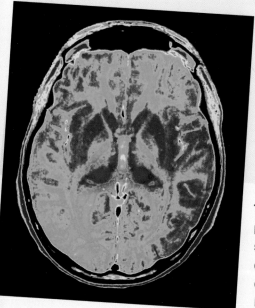

This is a brain scan from a 17-year-old patient who died from vCJD. The red spots are the areas affected by the disease. This illness destroys nerve cells and causes brain tissue to become spongy.

# Cow Hunt!

**Could one sick cow really trigger a food disaster? It could if it were fed to other cows.**

Hughes knew that the meat from a single cow couldn't make very many people sick. The real danger was if the disease was passed to other cows.

How could that happen? After cows are slaughtered, the parts you can eat go to meat processing plants to be made into hamburger and steaks. The parts you can't eat—like the bones and hooves—are often sent to factories that grind them into meal for animal feed.

This is a cow brain that is being tested for disease. Many countries do random tests on cow parts to determine if deadly diseases are present. The diseased cow in Washington State was discovered during random testing.

So the infected parts of the sick cow, like the brain and spinal cord, could have been put in the feed. If so, the disease could spread from herd to herd, creating a mad cow epidemic, or widespread outbreak.

Hughes studied the report to learn the facts of the case.

A few hours before Hughes received the call about the infected meat, a U.S. Department of Agriculture (**USDA**) scientist in Iowa had done a random test on some cow tissue. He

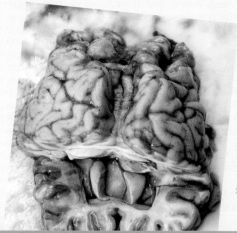

# THAT'S OFFAL

**These parts of the cow are banned from the food chain.**

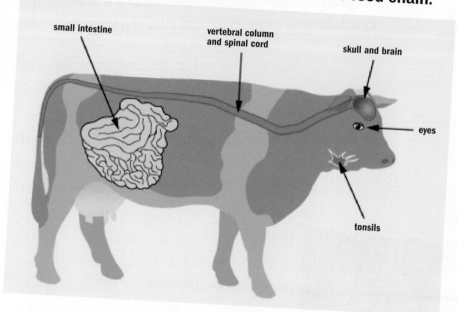

small intestine

vertebral column
and spinal cord

skull and brain

eyes

tonsils

looked into a microscope and saw a bright red stain on a slice of gray brain tissue. That's a sure sign of mad cow disease.

The scientist checked his records. The sample came from a Holstein, a black and white dairy cow. She lived in Canada for most of her life. That's probably where she got infected. But no one noticed, and she was later sold to a ranch in Washington State.

After the cow was killed, she was cut up. Then various parts of her body were sent to factories in three western states.

Now Hughes knew what he was looking for—and where to start.

This diagram shows the parts of a cow that are at high risk for carrying BSE. Federal agencies have banned these parts from the human food supply.

# Hoofing It

**Hughes and other investigators work around the clock to track the infected cow parts.**

Hughes and other investigators from the FDA began tracking the cow's parts through Washington, Oregon, and Idaho.

For 32 days, they drove along icy roads in the middle of the night. They logged thousands of miles and battled fierce snowstorms. They slept in little motels and ate at truck stops.

A meat market in Paris, France. The meat industry always takes a hard hit when cases of mad cow disease are discovered.

Some trudged through muddy farms and feed mills. Others picked through **carcasses** in slaughterhouses. Some pulled bad burgers from grocery store shelves. At night, they talked on the phone and compared the day's results.

Hughes was assigned to find infected cow parts at meat processing plants in Washington. He remembers the sad look on some owners' faces when he flashed his badge. If there was a chance that any of their meat might have mad cow, they'd have to throw it *all* away.

"The business they built from scratch was destroyed—through no fault of their own. And there was nothing they could do about it," Hughes says.

Some plant owners asked him to destroy their meat quietly. They didn't want the word to get out. "Once your name gets mixed up with mad cow, no one ever wants to buy your meat again," he says.

By February, about 2,000 tons of cattle byproducts were destroyed. Investigators had examined 75,000 cattle in three states—and killed 255 of them to test for BSE. (You can't test for BSE on a live cow.) They didn't find another sick cow.

Still, the investigators were confident they had saved the food supply from mad cow

Cattle must be killed before they can be tested for BSE. Here, cattle in Great Britain that had been tested for BSE infection are buried.

disease. After all, they had tracked down the diseased cow's body parts—and then destroyed them.

But the process had cost many animals' lives—and many people's businesses and jobs. "When I look back at all the people who were affected by this one cow," Hughes says, "it's just heartbreaking."

# The Mad Cow Mystery

**Could mad cow strike again? And would it be worse next time?**

Hughes and his team had prevented a health disaster. They recovered enough of the sick cow to stop an outbreak of mad cow disease. It had taken the team more than a month. "This wasn't exactly like finding a needle in a haystack, but it was pretty close," he says.

Between February 2004 and February 2007, two more cows in the U.S. tested positive for mad cow disease. In both cases, their meat products were recovered before anyone got sick.

But the thought of a mad cow epidemic still keeps Hughes awake some nights.

He's now the BSE coordinator in the Seattle district. His job is to prevent a mad cow outbreak.

Hughes has inspected everything from trucks that haul beef to pet food manufacturers who use trimmings from cow parts in dog food. Some days you'll find him slogging through muddy dairy farms, inspecting cows. Other days, he'll be on conference calls with meat importers, teaching them how to spot sick cattle.

"There's a lot of beef out there," he says. "We have to make sure that every scrap is safe—whether it shows up in a feed mill or on your dinner table." **24/7**

A no-trespassing sign was posted at the dairy farm in Washington State where the diseased cow had been found. The other cows at this farm were placed in quarantine.

# IS YOUR FOOD SAFE FROM MAD COW?

## Government experts say you shouldn't worry about your beef.

Can a steak or hamburger that's infected with mad cow disease end up on your dinner plate?

The answer is: Probably not.

Since the disease first appeared in England in 1986, governments have tightened their rules to keep sick cows out of the food supply. But it's such a huge effort that it's impossible to catch all bad beef, experts say.

Most cows become infected by eating feed that contains parts from sick animals. The FDA has banned the use of cow and sheep parts in cattle feed. But there are loopholes. Parts from ground-up cows are still used in feed for chickens and pigs. Those animals can then be made into feed for cows.

### A Test for Meat

Each country tests slaughtered cows for disease, but at different rates. Japan, for example, tests a sample from every cow that will be used for food. The meat is kept in refrigerators until the test comes back negative. Most European nations test about 70 percent of their cows.

But in the U.S., only about 650,000 of the 35 million cattle slaughtered each year are tested. That's less than one percent.

Some consumer groups have called for more testing and better detection safeguards. But the USDA says the food supply is safe. The chances of humans getting mad cow disease are still very, very low.

An inspector from the USDA checks out some meat.

# MEDICAL DOWNLOAD

Here's even more amazing stuff about animal diseases for you to digest.

## IN THIS SECTION:

▶ a mystery disease that killed 50 million people;

▶ how disease hunters have been in the news;

▶ the tools that are used to study and treat diseases;

▶ and whether being an epidemiologist might be in your future.

### 1918 The Superbug

A deadly influenza bug—called the Spanish flu—kills 40 to 50 million people across the globe (*right*). More than 500,000 Americans die. The flu is spread by soldiers returning home from World War I. Scientists still aren't sure where the killer bug came from—or where it went. It disappeared in 1919.

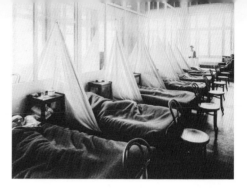

### 1957 Asian Flu

First found in China, the Asian flu causes 70,000 deaths in the United States. Unlike the Spanish flu, this bug is quickly identified. A life-saving vaccine is made available within months.

# Key Dates in the History

### 1996 A Bad Burger

Peter Hall, a 20-year-old vegetarian, dies of variant Creutzfeldt-Jakob disease (vCJD). A British coroner rules that Hall caught it from eating bad burgers as a child. The ruling is the first to link a human death to mad cow disease.

### 1968 Another Pandemic

The Hong Kong flu becomes a major flu pandemic, or global killer. More than 34,000 Americans die. This bug is similar to the Asian flu of 1957. Scientists believe fewer people are killed by this strain because they've developed a natural immunity, or defense, to it.

### 1986 Don't Eat the Meat

The first diagnosis of bovine spongiform encephalopathy (BSE)—or mad cow disease—is made in Britain. In the next five years, mad cow will appear in much of Europe, including Spain, Italy, and Greece.

# of Disease

**Deadly flu bugs and mad cow disease are nothing new. Look back in time to see when they first appeared.**

### 1997 When Birds Get Flu . . .

In Hong Kong, bird flu is first found in humans. The virus infects 18 people, and six die. Fortunately, the bug was not spread from person to person.

### 2003 . . . And Cows Go Mad!

The first U.S. case of mad cow disease is confirmed. It's found in an infected Canadian cow that had been slaughtered in Washington State. Days later, the government announces new restrictions to improve the safety of American beef.

See Case #2!

# Spanish Flu Mystery May Be Solved!

ATLANTA—October 5, 2005

A team of scientists has solved an 87-year-old mystery. The cause of the 1918 Spanish flu, which killed 40 to 50 million people, has finally been identified. A bird flu virus had jumped to humans.

Scientists from the U.S. Armed Forces Institute of Pathology studied samples from victims of the Spanish flu. Eventually, they were able to re-create the virus. They learned that it was similar to the current bird flu virus.

Dr. Julie Gerberding, director of the CDC, told the British Broadcasting Company (BBC), "By unmasking the 1918 virus, we are revealing some of the secrets that will help us prepare for the next pandemic."

Added John Oxford of the Royal London Hospital: "It's a huge breakthrough to be able to put a searchlight on a virus that killed millions of people."

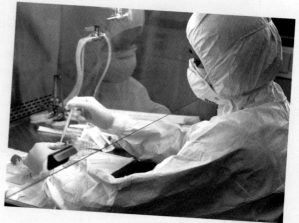

A scientist studies influenza virus cells at the WHO National Influenza Center. Scientists continue studying the Spanish flu virus to find out what it can teach them about contemporary outbreaks.

Students in Toronto march during the 2006 World AIDS Day. The day is now organized by the World AIDS Campaign, with the goal of increasing awareness of AIDS. The group's slogan is carried by the students: "Stop AIDS. Keep the Promise."

# People Observe World AIDS Day!

December 1, 2006

People all over the globe are observing World AIDS Day on December 1, 2006. World AIDS Day was established by the World Health Association in 1988. Every December 1, governments, churches, community organizations, and individuals show their support for the fight against the widespread disease of **HIV/ AIDS**. (HIV is the virus that causes AIDS.)

More than 25 million people worldwide have died of the AIDS pandemic since 1981. And nearly 40 million more now live with the disease. Some 40,000 new infections occur every year.

AIDS is growing fastest in the poorest countries of Africa. These nations don't have enough doctors, medical labs, or money for medicine. A recent study showed that only a small percentage of HIV-infected children in Africa are getting any medical treatment at all.

# The Disease Hunter's Toolbox

**From biohazard suits to super computers, infectious disease fighters need lots of equipment.**

*biohazard suit* These outfits protect against viruses and dangerous biological or chemical threats. Epidemiologists wore biohazard suits while fighting the Ebola virus in Africa. They also wore them while investigating the SARS mystery in Asia.

*masks* Masks are a must for fighting airborne illnesses like SARS, Ebola, and bird flu. The best ones are called N-95 respirators. They keep out tiny particles, like droplets of lung fluid from coughing patients.

*goggles* Goggles protect disease hunters' eyes from contaminated blood, saliva, parasites, and other dangerous objects.

*gloves* Doctors and scientists use different types of gloves. Surgical gloves help keep a wound **sterile**—free from dangerous germs and **bacteria**. Examination gloves prevent contamination or infection when treating a patient.

*microscope* A microscope is used to study things that are too small for the eye to see. It has a lens that magnifies objects to make them visible. Scientists use a microscope to study brain tissue from diseased cows or blood samples from bird flu patients.

*syringe* A syringe is used for giving injections and for taking blood. It is a tube with a plunger and a hollow needle attached.

*gowns* Health experts use different types of gowns. Surgical gowns are used in the operating room to keep everything sterile—free from germs and bacteria. Isolation gowns keep sick patients from spreading infected substances, like tiny drops of body fluid.

*super computers* Virologists use super computers to analyze the complicated genetic structure of viruses. The computers can also track every time a virus mutates.

*slides* Slides are small, thin pieces of glass. Technicians smear samples of blood or tissue on them, then study the slides under a microscope.

# Fear of Food?

## Don't worry about mad cow disease. But pay attention to E. coli.

We want you to enjoy your food. Really, we do. But there could be some nasty bacteria lurking in that burger. Or in that salad.

That bacteria is called **E. coli** 0157:H7. It can cause severe stomachaches, vomiting, and diarrhea.

E. coli 0157:H7 is generally spread from undercooked meat. But you can also get it from drinking raw milk, unpasteurized apple juice, or unchlorinated water. And—very rarely— it can appear in fresh, leafy vegetables that have been exposed to water contaminated by manure.

Here's how you can protect yourself from it.

### 1. Wash Your Hands Carefully
Proper hand washing can get rid of almost half of all foodborne illnesses. Always wash your hands before and after you handle food, eat a meal, use the bathroom, change a baby's diaper, touch raw food, touch an animal, sneeze or cough, handle garbage, or touch an open sore.

### 2. Don't Cross-Contaminate
When raw meat comes in contact with other foods, it can cause **cross-contamination**. Don't use the same utensils for meat and other foods. And be sure to wipe down countertops and cutting boards. Store raw meat on the bottom shelf of your refrigerator so it doesn't drip onto other food.

### 3. Keep Hot Foods Hot
Harmful bacteria are destroyed by cooking food properly. Beware of raw or partly cooked meat.

### 4. Keep Cold Foods Cold
Meat, fish, milk, and eggs should be kept cold. And don't defrost frozen food at room temperature. Thaw it in the refrigerator overnight, under cold running water, or in the microwave.

### 5. Wash Fruits and Vegetables
And keep in mind that washing may not remove all contamination. Public service announcements on TV, radio, or in the newspapers will tell you which foods to avoid in the event of an outbreak.

# A Modern Pandemic

**During the past 25 years, AIDS has spread throughout the world.**

The first cases of AIDS were reported in 1981. Since then, the disease has become a pandemic. Now there are nearly 40 million people infected with HIV, the virus that causes AIDS.

Africa is the hardest-hit continent. More than 60 percent of all the people in the world with HIV live there. But no region has been spared. The graph and map on these pages will tell you more.

## HIV/AIDS IN AFRICA

**The deadly disease has been dramatically shortening life expectancy.**

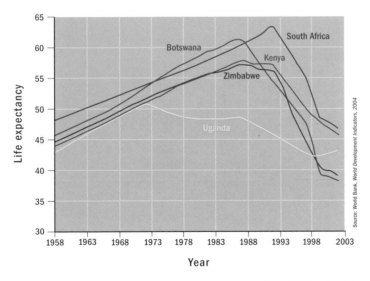

Source: World Bank, World Development Indicators, 2004

**HIV/AIDS has devastated the poorest countries of Africa. In the 11 nations with the highest rates of infection, the average human life span is just 47.7 years. That's 11 years less than it would be without the disease. Many people die because medical treatment is often poor or nonexistent.**

# HIV AROUND THE WORLD

**HIV/AIDS has affected every part of the world. Here's a look at the disease's toll in 2006.**

**Western and Central Europe**
adults and children living with HIV: 740,000

adult and child deaths due to HIV: 12,000

**North America**
adults and children living with HIV: 1.4 million

adult and child deaths due to HIV: 18,000

**Western and Central Europe**

**North America**

**Caribbean**
adults and children living with HIV: 250,000

adult and child deaths due to HIV: 19,000

**Latin America**

**Latin America**
adults and children living with HIV: 1.7 million

adult and child deaths due to HIV: 65,000

**Middle East and North Africa**
adults and children living with HIV: 460,000

adult and child deaths due to HIV: 36,000

*Source: Joint United Nations Programme on HIV/AIDS (UNAIDS) and World Health Organization (WHO), 2006.*

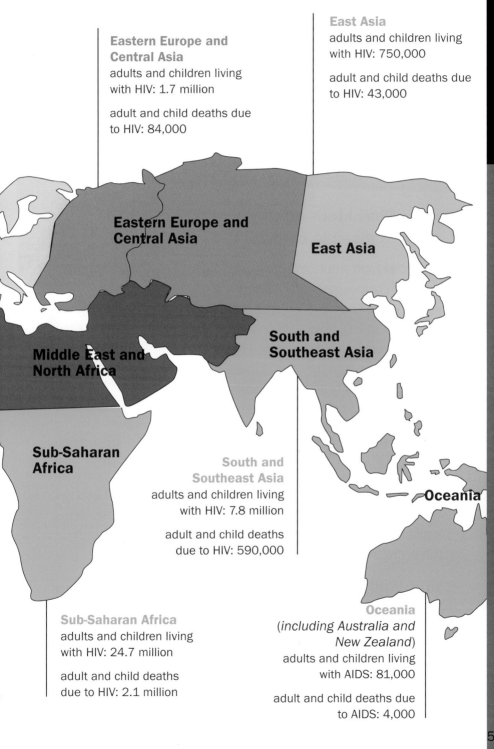

East Asia
adults and children living
with HIV: 750,000

adult and child deaths due
to HIV: 43,000

Eastern Europe and
Central Asia
adults and children living
with HIV: 1.7 million

adult and child deaths due
to HIV: 84,000

**Eastern Europe and
Central Asia**

**East Asia**

**Middle East and
North Africa**

**South and
Southeast Asia**

**Sub-Saharan
Africa**

South and
Southeast Asia
adults and children living
with HIV: 7.8 million

adult and child deaths
due to HIV: 590,000

**Oceania**

Sub-Saharan Africa
adults and children living
with HIV: 24.7 million

adult and child deaths
due to HIV: 2.1 million

Oceania
(*including Australia and
New Zealand*)
adults and children living
with AIDS: 81,000

adult and child deaths due
to AIDS: 4,000

# HELP WANTED:
# Epidemiologist

**Think studying the spread of disease could be infectious? Here's more information about the field.**

Dr. Scott Dowell is an epidemiologist at the Centers for Disease Control and Prevention (CDC) in Atlanta, Georgia.

**24/7:** What kinds of careers are there in disease control?

**DR. SCOTT DOWELL:** Many types. I'm an epidemiologist. That means I investigate the spread and control of diseases in big populations. Or you could become a virologist. That's a microbiologist who specializes in viruses. If you're interested in animal diseases, you could become a veterinarian.

**24/7:** How did you become interested in disease control?

**DR. DOWELL:** My father was a doctor. I remember being very young and traveling with him and my mother to Haiti. He treated patients there who were suffering from different viruses.

**24/7:** And working with the CDC has allowed you to do that?

**DR. DOWELL:** Right. I joined the CDC as an epidemic intelligence service officer. We're like medical detectives. We're the ones who run to a country when we hear about an outbreak of disease. Usually, the nation's government asks us for help. Their people are dying and they need outside aid.

**24/7:** The diseases sound awfully dangerous. Is your job scary?

**DR. DOWELL:** The truth is, most of the places I go are not as dangerous as they seem in movies. The diseases are often deadly, but we take many precautions to keep ourselves safe. I travel with my family to most sites. It can be a great adventure. And it's a chance to see different parts of the world.

**24/7:** Are there some places that are too dangerous to take your family?

## THE STATS

**DAY JOB:** About half of all epidemiologists work for the government. Another 12 percent work for scientific and technical consulting firms. And 8 percent work in private hospitals.

**MONEY:** The average salary for an epidemiologist is $54,800. But they can make over $80,000.

**EDUCATION:** The minimum education an epidemiologist can have is:
▶ 4 years of college
▶ a master's degree from a school of public health
Most epidemiologists also earn a PhD or a medical degree.

**THE NUMBERS:** There are about 4,800 epidemiologists working today around the world.

**DR. DOWELL:** Yes. A good friend died when we treated Ebola in Uganda. Another friend died when we fought SARS in Thailand. I spent time in Zaire treating Ebola. It was so dangerous that I wore a protective spacesuit. We were in a poor hospital with very little equipment. We walked through troughs filled with bleach to get the virus off our shoes.

**24/7:** What have you learned about controlling disease?

**DR. DOWELL:** It's a simple lesson. Wealthy countries like the U.S. need to work with poorer ones. We've seen diseases spread out of control in nations that don't have good public health systems. You can tell yourself that what happens in Thailand or Zaire doesn't matter here. But it's a small world.

# DO YOU HAVE WHAT IT TAKES?

## Take this totally unscientific quiz to find out if disease hunting might be a good career for you.

**1 How do you feel about science class?**

a) I stay after school to look at microscope slides.

b) I'm doing well, but I'd rather be at lunch.

c) I wouldn't know. I've slept through every class.

**2 Are you good at explaining things to people?**

a) Absolutely. I can explain anything to anyone.

b) I'll never be a teacher, but I help my friends learn certain things.

c) I can barely understand things myself half the time.

**3 Are you good in an emergency?**

a) Yes, I've got a level head.

b) Sometimes yes, sometimes no.

c) Help! Get me out of here!

**4 I think the best way to deal with sick people, is . . .**

a) Do everything I can to take care of them.

b) Be cautious, but help if I can.

c) Run to another room. Or building. Or state.

**5 How do you feel about foreign cultures?**

a) Fascinating! I love to learn about other countries.

b) I prefer my hometown, but I'm curious about them.

c) I'm happy just knowing about where I live.

### YOUR SCORE

Give yourself 3 points for every "a" you chose. Give yourself 2 points for every "b" you chose. Give yourself 1 point for every "c" you chose.

If you got **13–15** points, you're a born disease hunter!

If you got **10–12** points, disease hunting is a career option.

If you got **5–9** points, you might want to look at another career.

54

# HOW TO GET STARTED...NOW!

**It's never too early to start working toward your goals.**

## GET AN EDUCATION

▶ Starting now, take as many biology, chemistry, physics, health, math, and computer classes as you can. Social studies classes are also important to learn about different countries and cultures.

▶ Train yourself to ask questions, gather new information, and make conclusions.

▶ Start thinking about college. Look for ones that have good science programs. Call or write to those colleges to get information.

▶ Read the newspaper. The headlines are filled with stories about bird flu, mad cow, and diseases like Ebola and SARS.

▶ Read anything you can about infectious diseases. Learn about historical and recent cases. See the books and Web sites in the Resources section on pages 56–58.

▶ Graduate from high school!

## NETWORK!

Ask your own doctor for advice about becoming an epidemiologist or infectious disease doctor. Get in touch with your local hospital. Ask if you can interview an epidemiologist or infectious disease doctor.

## GET AN INTERNSHIP

Call your local hospital or doctors' offices. And ask your school's science teachers. There might be internships available. It doesn't hurt to ask!

## LEARN ABOUT OTHER JOBS IN THE FIELD

There are many careers that study and treat infectious diseases. Here are some of them:

**biologist:** studies living organisms

**ecologist:** studies how organisms relate to the environment

**entomologist:** specializes in insects

**epidemiologist:** medical scientist who studies what causes, and how to control, epidemics

**infectious disease pharmacist:** specializes in putting formulas together and dispensing drugs with a focus on infectious disease medicines

**microbiologist:** studies microscopic cells in human illness

**parasitologist:** studies parasites

**pathologist:** studies disease, especially its effects on body tissue

**zoologist:** specializes in animal life

# Resources

## Looking for more information? Here are some resources you don't want to miss!

## SCHOOLS

**Johns Hopkins University**
www.jhu.edu
Admissions Office
615 N. Wolfe Street, Suite E1002
Baltimore, MD 21205
**PHONE:** 410-955-3543
**E-MAIL:** admiss@jhs.edu

This college also offers a terrific public health school.

**University of California-Davis**
www.ucdavis.edu
Undergraduate Admissions
One Shields Avenue
Davis, CA 95616-8507
**PHONE:** 530-752-2971

This college has a world-renowned public health and veterinary school.

**University of Illinois at Chicago**
www.uic.edu
Office of Admissions and Records
1200 West Harrison Street
Chicago, IL 60607-7161
**PHONE:** 312-996-4350

The university's College of Applied Health Sciences is a leader in the field.

**University of Nebraska-Lincoln**
www.unl.edu
1410 Q Street
P.O. Box 880417
Lincoln, NE 68588-041
**PHONE:** 800-742-8800
**E-MAIL:** admissions@unl.edu

This Midwest school has one of the finest agricultural colleges in the country.

**University of Pennsylvania**
www.vet.upenn.edu
School of Veterinary Medicine
3800 Spruce Street
Philadelphia, PA 19104
**PHONE:** 215-898-5434
**E-MAIL:** admissions@vet.upenn.edu

This Ivy League university has a great veterinary program.

**University of Toronto**
www.utoronto.ca
25 Kings College Circle
Toronto, Ontario, Canada M5S 1A1
**PHONE:** 416-978-5000
**E-MAIL:** information.commons @utoronto.ca

This university is one of Canada's finest science schools.

# PROFESSIONAL ORGANIZATIONS

## Centers for Disease Control and Prevention (CDC)
www.jhu.edu
1600 Clifton Road
Atlanta, GA 30333
**PHONE:** 800-311-3435

The CDC was founded in 1946, primarily to fight malaria. It is part of the Department of Health and Human Services. Today, the group is a leader in efforts to prevent and control disease, injuries, workplace hazards, and environmental and health threats.

## Infectious Diseases Society of America (IDSA)
www.idsociety.org
66 Canal Center Plaza, Suite 600
Alexandria, VA 22324
**PHONE:** 703-299-0200
**FAX:** 703-299-0204
**E-MAIL:** info@idsociety.org

The IDSA represents physicians, scientists, and other health-care professionals who specialize in infectious diseases. The society's purpose is to improve the health of individuals, communities, and society by promoting excellence in patient care, education, research, public health, and prevention relating to infectious diseases.

## International Society for Infectious Diseases (ISID)
www.isid.org
1330 Beacon Street, Suite 228
Brookline MA 02446
**PHONE:** 617-277-0551
**FAX:** 617-278-9113
**E-MAIL:** info@isid.org

The ISID is committed to improving the care of patients with infectious diseases, the training of clinicians and researchers in infectious diseases and microbiology, and the control of infectious diseases around the world.

## National Institute of Allergy and Infectious Disease (NIAID)
www3.niaid.nih.gov/
6610 Rockledge Drive, MSC 612
Bethesda, MD 20892
**PHONE:** 301-496-5717

For more than 50 years, NIAID has conducted research that helps treat, prevent, and better understand infectious and other diseases. It is part of the National Institutes of Health.

# WEB SITES

### FDA
www.fda.gov

This site provides the latest news in food safety and approved medications.

### Flu Factoids
pbskids.org/zoom/fromyou/survey/flu_facts.html

Find out cool news about the flu— and ways to avoid it—at this PBS site.

### U.S. Department of Agriculture
www.ars.usda.gov

Look here for updated information about food safety.

### Web MD
www.webmd.com

This is a comprehensive, easy-to-use site with all sorts of helpful medical information.

### World Health Organization
www.who.int/en/

This international organization offers infectious disease information in English, French, and Spanish.

# BOOKS

Emmeluth, Donald. *Influenza* (Deadly Diseases and Epidemics). Broomall, Pa.: Chelsea House, 2003.

Gave, Marc, and Lynn Brunelle, eds. *Viruses* (Discovery Channel School Science). Milwaukee: Gareth Stevens Publishing, 2003.

Getz, David. *Purple Death: The Mysterious Flu of 1918.* New York: Henry Holt, 2000.

Goldstein, Natalie. *Viruses* (Germs! The Library of Disease-Causing Organisms). New York: Rosen Publishing Group, 2004.

Grady, Denise. *Deadly Invaders: Virus Outbreaks Around the World, from Marburg Fever to Avian Flu* (A New York Times Book). New York: Kingfisher, 2006.

Monroe, Judy. *Influenza and Other Viruses* (Perspectives on Disease and Illness). Mankato, Minn.: Capstone Press, 2001.

Orr, Tamra. *Avian Flu* (Coping in a Changing World). New York: Rosen Publishing, 2007.

# A

**AIDS** (aydz) *noun* a disease that causes the human immune system to break down and lower resistance to deadly diseases. It's short for *acquired immune deficiency syndrome.*

**antiviral** (AN-tih-vye-ral) *adjective* capable of destroying or weakening a virus

**avian influenza** (AYE-vee-un in-floo-EN-zuh) *noun* a highly contagious virus that usually strikes poultry, like chickens and turkeys; it has also been known to infect people. It is commonly known as bird flu.

# B

**bacteria** (bak-TEER-ee-uh) *noun* a microscopic one-celled organism. Some bacteria are essential for our survival and others may cause disease.

**biohazard suit** (bye-oh-HAZ-urd soot) *noun* a full body suit that scientists and investigators wear in order to protect themselves from infection and disease

**bovine spongiform encephalopathy (BSE)** (BOH-vine SPUHN-ji-form en-SEH-fah-LAH-path-ee) *noun* a deadly brain disease that usually affects cattle, but has also struck humans. It is commonly known as mad cow disease.

# C

**carcasses** (KAR-kahs-ez) *noun* dead bodies

**CDC** (SEE-dee-see) *noun* a U.S. government agency that studies infectious diseases. It's short for the *Centers for Disease Control and Prevention.*

**cremated** (KREE-mayte-ehd) *adjective* describing a dead body that has been burned and reduced to ashes

**cross-contamination** (kraws kuhn-tam-uh-NAY-shuhn) *noun* the instance of mixing infected food with noninfected food and then spreading the infection

# D

**dementia** (deh-MEN-shuh) *noun* a neurological disorder that causes loss of perception, memory, and judgment

**diagnosis** (dye-ugh-NOHS-sis) *noun* an identification of a patient's illness by getting lab tests and studying physical symptoms

**Dictionary**

# E

**Ebola** (ee-BOH-lah) *noun* a highly contagious infectious disease caused by an airborne virus. It was first noticed in Africa.

**E. coli** (ee KOH-lye) *noun* a species of bacteria that is usually found in the intestines of humans and other animals. While internal E. coli is harmless and helpful in digestion, eating or drinking outside E. coli (like polluted water or meat that has not been processed safely) can cause severe food poisoning.

**epidemic** (ep-uh-DEM-ik) *noun* an outbreak of disease that spreads quickly over a wide area and to many people

**epidemiologists** (ep-uh-dee-mee-OHL-uh-jists) *noun* scientists who study the patterns and causes of disease, and control disease in groups of people

# F

**FDA** (ef-dee-AYE) *noun* the U.S. government agency responsible for the safety and effectiveness of foods, drugs, vaccines, and medical devices. It's short for *Food and Drug Administration*.

# H

**H5N1** *noun* a deadly variety of bird flu that is currently affecting people in Asia.

**HIV** (aych-eye-VEE) *noun* a retro virus that causes AIDS. It's short for *human immunodeficiency virus*.

**hot zone** (hot zohn) *noun* a place where a disease has been detected and there's a high danger of catching it

# I

**immunity** (ih-MYOO-nih-tee) *noun* the condition of being able to resist getting a certain disease

**infectious** (in-FEK-shuhss) *adjective* easy to spread from one person to another

# M

**mutate** (MYOO-tate) *verb* to change the genetic material of a cell

# O

**offal** (AWH-fuhl) *noun* the internal organs of an animal

**outbreak** (OUT-brake) *noun* the spread of disease in a short period of time and in a limited population

# P

**pandemic** (pan-DEM-ik) *noun* an outbreak of disease that spreads to many different countries or throughout the world

**prognosis** (prog-NOH-sis) *noun* a prediction about a patient's recovery from an illness

# Q

**quarantine** (KWOR-uhn-teen) *noun* the process of keeping people or animals who could become sick away from healthy ones; this helps to prevent further spread of the disease

# S

**sanitation** (san-uh-TAY-shuhn) *noun* a system for cleaning the water supply and disposing of sewage or bacteria

**SARS** (sars) *noun* a contagious and sometimes fatal respiratory illness that has spread worldwide. It resembles pneumonia or influenza. It's short for *severe acute respiratory syndrome*.

**secretions** (suh-KREE-shuhns) *noun* materials, such as saliva, that are released by plants and animals

**Spanish flu** (SPAN-ish floo) *noun* a deadly virus that killed between 40 and 50 million people from 1918 to 1919

**sterile** (STEH-ruhl) *adjective* free from dangerous germs or bacteria

**strain** (strayn) *noun* a specific version or type of a bacteria or virus

**symptoms** (SIMP-tuhmz) *noun* physical signs of illness

# U

**USDA** (yoo-ess-DEE-aye) *noun* the U.S. government agency that monitors the food supply. It's short for *United States Department of Agriculture*.

# V

**vaccine** (vak-SEEN) *noun* an injection given to prevent a specific illness. It's usually made from a very weakened version of the disease so the body can learn to fight it off.

**virus** (VYE-ruhss) *noun* a tiny organism that often causes disease

# Index

Africa, 19, 45, 49, *49*, 50
AIDS virus. See HIV/AIDS.
antiviral medicines, 10, 24, *24*
Asian Flu, 42, *42*, 43
Atlanta, Georgia, 18, 20
avian influenza. See bird flu.

Bangkok, Thailand, 23, *26*
biohazard suits, 19, 46, *46*, 53
biologists, 52, 55
bird flu, 10, *10*, 16, 18, *18*, 19,
        21–22, *21*, 22–24, *23*,
        25–28, 43–46, 55
Bovine Spongiform Encephalopathy
        (BSE). See mad cow disease.
British Broadcasting Company
        (BBC), 44

carcasses, 36
Centers for Disease Control and
        Prevention (CDC), 18, 20,
        44, 52
cholera, 20
conclusions, 14, 55
cremation, 22
Creutzfeldt-Jakob disease, 11,
        33, 42

DDT (pesticide), 20
dementia, 33
diagnoses, 9, 12, 43
Dowell, Scott, 16, 18–19, *19*,
        21–24, 27, 52–53, *52*

E. coli, 48
Ebola, 19, 46, 53, 55
ecologists, 55
education, 53, 55
entomologists, 55
epidemics, 8, 20, 34, 39

epidemiologists, 12, 18, 46,
        52–53, 55
evidence, 14, 22, 23

Food and Drug Administration
        (FDA), 31, 36, 40
food investigators, 12
Fort Collins, Colorado, 20

Gerberding, Julie, 44
gloves, 46
goggles, 46
gowns, 47

H5N1 strain, 22, 26, 27
Hall, Peter, 42
HIV/AIDS, 20, 45, 49, *49*, 50–51,
        *50–51*
Hong Kong flu, 43, *43*
hot zones, 9, 22
Hughes, Will, 31–32, 34–39

immunity, 25, 43
infectious disease pharmacists, 55
insecticides, 20
inspections, 12, 36, 39, 40, *40*
internal medicine doctors, 12
internships, 55

mad cow disease, 11, *11*, 31–32,
        33, 34–35, *34*, *35*, 36–40,
        42–43
malaria, 20
masks, 19, 46, *46*
medicines, 24, *24*, 25, 26, 27, 55
microbiologists, 55
microscopes, 26, 34, 47, *47*
mutations, 9, 23, 25–27

N-95 respirators, 46
National Influenza Center, *44*

outbreaks, 8, 9, 20–21, *21*, 28, 34,
        38–39, 49, 52
Oxford, John, 44

pandemics, 9, 19, 22, 27, 28, 43,
        44, 45, 49

62

# Author's Note

**K**iller chickens? Crazy cows? The subjects in this book can sound pretty scary. Researching and writing these stories, I began to think I might never eat a burger again.

But this book isn't meant to frighten you. Most of what you eat is perfectly safe. There's no reason to fear your cheeseburger and fries. Or your mom's fried chicken.

But there are some lessons you can take from this book. First, be aware that these diseases are out there and that you might be able to help fight them. Dr. Scott Dowell thinks the whole world should help poor countries battle diseases like bird flu. That makes a lot of sense. A disease that hatches in a little town halfway across the world can find its way to our front door.

Second, think about how you can stay healthy. We've given you tips for cooking, cleaning, and eating. But the best advice is simple common sense. Wash your hands. Stay away from sick people. And if you've got a cold, stay in bed.

While writing this book, I visited libraries and Web sites. I read books and articles. But the best way to get good information is to go right to the source. No, not the birds and cows. The scientists. A lot of dedicated people spent a lot of hours talking to me about how they do their work. Without their help, this book wouldn't be possible.

**CONTENT ADVISER:** Mark S. Dworkin, MD, MPH & TM, Associate Professor, Division of Epidemiology and Biostatistics, University of Illinois at Chicago

Guthrie Memorial Library
Hanover's Public Library
Hanover, PA 17331-2283